Steve Nash: The Inspiring Story of One of Basketball's Greatest Point Guards

An Unauthorized Biography

GW00499681

By: Clayton Geoffreys

Visit my website at www.claytongeoffreys.com
Cover photo by Keith Allison is licensed under CC BY 2.0 / modified from original

Table of Contents

Foreword

Growing up, there were few point guards more exciting to watch than Steve Nash. A true master of his craft and an all-around class act, Steve Nash embodies what it means to be a role model for youth everywhere. Watching Nash from his early years in Dallas to his prime in Phoenix, it was unbelievable to see a man who many thought would never last in the National Basketball Association, prove all of his doubters wrong. When Mark Cuban decided to not resign Nash when he became a free-agent because most point guards begin to fade once they hit their 30s, Steve Nash moved on to Phoenix to prove Mark and his other critics wrong. Over and over in his career, Steve Nash has silenced those who have counted him out. His story is truly one of inspiration. Thank you for purchasing *Steve Nash: The Inspiring Story of One of Basketball's Greatest Point Guards*. In this unauthorized biography, we will learn Steve Nash's incredible life story and impact on the game of basketball. Hope you enjoy and if you do, please do not forget to leave a review!

Also, check out my website at claytongeoffreys.com to join my exclusive list where I let you know about my latest books. To thank you for your purchase, you can go to my site to download a free copy of *33 Life Lessons: Success Principles, Career Advice & Habits of Successful People*. In the book, you'll learn from some of the greatest thought leaders of different industries on what it takes to become successful and how to live a great life.

Cheers,

Clayton Geoffreys

Visit me at www.claytongeoffreys.com

33 LIFE LESSONS

SUCCESS PRINCIPLES, CAREER ADVICE
& HABITS OF SUCCESSFUL PEOPLE

CLAYTON GEOFFREYS

Introduction

When you talk about the best passing point guards in NBA history, legendary players like Magic Johnson, John Stockton, Isiah Thomas, and Jason Kidd come into mind. All of the above-mentioned players have been All-Stars (or even superstars) in their careers and have all been tasked to run their team's offense. But one point guard deserves a lot of attention and recognition for what he has done in the NBA by simply running a team's offense. That point guard goes by the name of Steve Nash.

Unlike most other superstar point guards, Steve Nash was never highly regarded early in his life. He was underrated in high school and he even begged for college basketball tryouts at a time when high school stars never went through tryouts to enter a reputable college program. After getting his college degree and entering the NBA Draft, he was booed by the Phoenix Suns' fans after he was drafted in 1996 because of his not-so-stellar college career. Despite that, Steve Nash went on to become one of the best passers and playmakers in the NBA, and would also be recognized as the best player in the NBA for two straight seasons due to his ability to make plays for other people.

After figuratively kneeling in prayer just to play for a college basketball team and after being booed on his draft night, Steve Nash went on to become an eight-time All-Star, seven-time All-NBA Team member (two on the First Team, two on the Second Team, and three on the Third Team), and a five-time assists leader. He would also go on to win the most coveted individual award in the NBA—the regular season MVP—not only once but twice. One may wonder why and how Steve Nash was able to achieve all of those despite his unheralded entry into the NBA. Well, anybody will say that Nash worked extremely hard to get to where he is. While that remains a hundred percent true, what's even more true is that Nash got to where he is because of his natural leadership ability and his propensity for unselfish play in a sport where scoring gets you more attention than anything else.

Early in his NBA career in Phoenix, Steve Nash was just a third-string point guard behind two established playmakers, Kevin Johnson and Jason Kidd. Despite not seeing many minutes, he worked harder and harder until the Dallas

Mavericks gave him a chance to become a starter. That was when Nash began to show flashes of what he could become as a passer and a playmaker. He went on to become a two-time All-Star in Dallas but would later return to Phoenix, the team that shunned him early in his life, as an entirely different player. He had his best years in Phoenix while running an ultra high-scoring group of players whose main mission was to outscore opposing teams by as much as they could every single night.

In Phoenix, Nash became the MVP twice and developed into the league's best passing point guard. There was nobody who could run a team like Nash could and no other point guard could set up scoring opportunities for teammates better than the skinny MVP from Canada. He basically could win a game just by passing the ball. He seldom scored a lot of points because his basic nature was being an unselfish leader. But when he did score, Nash could not miss. While he earned his reputation by being an assists man, Nash is also one of the best and most efficient shooters in NBA history. He has a career field goal percentage of 49%, a career three-point percentage of almost 43%, and a free throw percentage of 90.4%. Those are all impressive numbers considering that Nash was never as big or as athletic as other players in the league. Nash went on to have successful winning years in Phoenix as he racked up the assists numbers and the individual accolades. But for all his flair and success in Phoenix, there was one thing that eluded him—the NBA championship. As great a player as he was, Steve Nash never won an NBA title in his career, nor did he even come close to winning it, even as his team finished as the best during the regular season. There have been a lot of great NBA players who have won MVPs and scoring titles but never won NBA championships. What makes Nash different from those players is that he was always an unselfish leader who made it a point to make other players better. His teammates weren't slackers; Nash played with great All-Stars such as Amar'e Stoudemire and Shawn Marion in their prime. This led people into thinking that his team's style of play could not win an NBA title. Despite the criticisms his coaches and his teammates faced for not delivering a title, Nash stayed loyal and in shape in order to try to win the trophy that eluded him for all of his life.

As loyal to the Suns as Steve Nash was, the team was going nowhere and they knew that their star point guard could get a better chance at winning a title elsewhere. He was then traded late into his career to the Los Angeles Lakers. At 38 years old, Nash was in the twilight of his career, but he had teammates such as Kobe Bryant, Pau Gasol, and Dwight Howard. Despite all the star power of his team, the Nash could never stay healthy and the Laker stars never gelled together.

Realizing his injuries could never get him back on the court playing at a high level of basketball, Steve Nash retired from the NBA after 18 seasons at the age of 39 years old. He now works for the Golden State Warriors as a part-time consultant and has been credited for mentoring a young Stephen Curry, whose offensive game resembles Nash's. For his career, Steve Nash averaged 14.3 points and 8.5 assists per game. He had a career total of 10,335 assists, which ranks third among the highest career assists totals in NBA history behind John Stockton and Jason Kidd.

Though Nash was never able to win a championship in his long NBA career, it is certain that he was one of the best point guards in basketball history. He changed the way the game was played at a time when the league was dominated by forwards like Tim Duncan, Kevin Garnett, Dirk Nowitzki, and LeBron James. Nash was as elite a point guard as any because he was able to get victories for his team just by passing the ball and controlling the tempo while other teams got the game rolling by throwing the ball into the post. As the league transitioned into a playmaker-dominated league in Nash's twilight years, one can credit that such a transformation was due to his success as a point guard. After all, when you're one of the best assists men in the history of the NBA, everybody would want to follow your lead.

Chapter 1: Childhood and Early Life

Before Steve Nash became a heralded NBA point guard and a practically guaranteed first-ballot Basketball Hall of Famer, he was just a child travelling all over the world. Stephen John Nash was born to John Nash, a professional soccer player, and Jean Nash in Johannesburg, South Africa, on February 7, 1974. From the beginning Steve and his younger brother, Martin, showed an affinity to sports.

The Nash family immigrated to Canada in 1976 to escape the South African apartheid. Prior to that, the elder Nash's profession was a reason for the family to travel all over the world. As a family, the Nash's participated in a number of different sports while Steve and Martin were growing up. Eventually, the Nash family settled down in Victoria, British Columbia, just miles away from the United States border.

Growing up, Steve and Martin both played a number of sports, including hockey, lacrosse, soccer, and tennis. Surprisingly, Steve did not play an organized game of basketball until he was in the eighth grade. Even though the Nash brothers were the sons of a professional athlete and their mom was a sports enthusiast, Steve's parents never forced their sons to play sports. At the same time though, they welcomed the idea of either of their sons following in John's footsteps.

As a child, it would have appeared to many that Steve Nash was destined for soccer greatness, just like his father. Steve possessed a feel for the game of soccer that one could only inherit, as it seemed genetic how natural he looked kicking the soccer ball; coupled with that trademark speed that many basketball enthusiasts have come to know and love whenever Nash commands the hardwood floors, Steve was a natural at soccer.

Steve, however, was a true athlete first and foremost and, like most Canadian boys growing up in his era, he looked up to the hockey great Wayne Gretzky. Nash, like Gretzky, believed in hard work as much as skill. It was due to Steve's hard work that he was named the Most Valuable Player in soccer for all of British Columbia as a junior in high school. In fact, Steve even received a spot on the

Canadian national team. Nash's natural gift at playing soccer and his development at that sport might have helped him in basketball. Soccer helps a player develop his footwork, which is very important in basketball. Above all, soccer players are trained to be able to see all over the vast soccer field. That part of his soccer training might be credited for his court vision in basketball.

Off the soccer field, Steve excelled at games of strategy, winning three chess tournaments while in elementary school. Looking back on that feat now, his early accomplishments as a chess player may have been a precursor to the way he dissected the defenses of opposing teams and saw through their strategies in college and later on in the NBA. Aside from soccer and from chess, Steve Nash was also a big fan of professional wrestling and was fond of watching legendary wrestlers such as Hulk Hogan. Nash was also very fond of lacrosse and rugby. He was indeed an avid fan of every kind of sport whether it was team-oriented, singles competition, or staged entertainment.

Steve Nash was first exposed to the sport of basketball prior to eighth grade and he played his first organized game in that grade. Nash loved the sport at first try just as much as he did with soccer. But there was something about the sport of basketball that made him more attracted to it, to the point that he declared to his family that he was going to be an NBA player in the future.

Ultimately, Steve Nash did not choose to become a professional soccer player like his father, but his brother Martin eventually would. To the surprise of anyone who may have known him growing up, Steve chose basketball and stuck with it. Given the lack of popularity in basketball in the area Steve grew up in, he would have seemingly had insurmountable odds stacked against him due to a lack of formidable competition and due to his skinny build; however, the future basketball great would not let a little thing like that deter him. The rest, as we all know, is history.

Chapter 2: The High School

High School Dominance in British Columbia

To start his high school basketball career, Steve Nash attended Mount Douglas Secondary School in Saanich, British Columbia. When the future NBA star began struggling in school, he was sent to St. Michael's University Boarding School in Victoria, British Columbia. While at St. Michael's, Nash not only starred in basketball, but he also played rugby and soccer. In eleventh grade, Steve Nash was named the Most Valuable Player in soccer for all of British Columbia, earning him a spot on the Canadian National soccer team. Nash, however, decided not to follow in his father John's footsteps; instead, he decided that he was going to play professional basketball in the National Basketball Association.

Despite being one of the best basketball players in British Columbia, averaging 21.3 points, 11.2 assists, and 9.1 rebounds a game, he did not draw the attention of any notable college basketball programs in the United States. His high school coach, Ian Hyde-Lay, was very impressed with how Nash played the game. His point guard could break ankles with his footwork and his ball handles above his deceptive quickness. Nash could also shoot very well for a player who just started playing the game a few years back. But the best facet of his game was that he always made it a point to make every one of his teammates better.

With that in mind, Hyde-Lay sent Nash's game tapes to every major college program of that time such as Duke, Villanova, Maryland, Arizona and Indiana. All of these notable college programs responded with, "Sorry, no thank you." Using these rejections as motivation, Steve stored all these rejection letters in a box in his closet. Despite these early setbacks, Steve still believed he could compete at the collegiate level among the best, especially after a summer visit to Long Beach, California, where he saw how he stacked up against some of the best talents available at the time.

Eventually, Steve's game tapes made their way into the hands of Coach Dick Davey at Santa Clara University, a Jesuit school in California. Davey's assistant Scott Gradin was the first to see the footage of Nash's play and was impressed by how he could easily make his defenders fall flat on their backside by using his quick feet and ball-handling skills. Dick Davey then flew up to the Great White North to see Nash play in person and was astonished at two things. The first thing was the fact that no other scouts were present to watch the young Canadian phenomenon and the second thing was how impressive the young point guard looked compared to his competition, even though the head coach knew that the competition in Canada was not the best. Steve would go on to sign with Santa Clara under the condition that he learned how to play defense, since Davey's biggest criticism of Nash at the time was that he was the "worst defensive player" he had ever seen. Though he would get better at that facet of the game, Steve Nash's defense was the most criticized part of his game even in the NBA.

Chapter 3: College Career

Freshman and Sophomore Seasons

Steve Nash enrolled at Santa Clara for the 1992-1993 NCAA season. Santa Clara was not a basketball powerhouse. For the five years prior to Nash's arrival, Santa Clara had failed to appear in the NCAA tournament. In fact, Santa Clara was not even a .500 team. It never had a reputation as a basketball school; and Santa Clara's best basketball product was the NBA champion Kurt Rambis. During his freshman campaign, things at Santa Clara would change with the young Steve Nash running the point.

For the 1992-1993 season, Santa Clara had perhaps their best recruiting class ever, with Steve Nash at the point and Academic All-American Pete Eisenrich, joined by a few other talented freshmen. Nash quickly became popular on campus for his jovial personality and quick smile. He was always naturally friendly as a person and that was one of the best qualities that made him a good leader. Reveling in college life and all that it had to offer, Nash could be found in the early morning hours in the gym, constantly working on his game. Basketball was his passion. It was his ticket to fulfilling his dream and to only way to do so was to work harder.

During his freshman years, Nash averaged 8.1 points, 2.2 assists, and 2.5 rebounds per game. Steve led the Santa Clara Broncos to a West Coast Conference championship, earning the school its first appearance in the NCAA tournament in five years. Nash was named the West Coast Conference tournament's Most Valuable Player, becoming the first freshman in conference history to win it.

In the NCAA tournament, the Broncos were first matched up against Arizona. Nobody would have ever imagined an upset potentially in the making, since the Broncos were seeded 15th in the March Madness tournament, but they were not a team that could be counted out just yet. On their part, Nash's team also did not expect much in their trip to the NCAA tourney. The Arizona game was a dogfight from the opening tipoff, but the Broncos were a fighting team led by an unknown, talented freshman guard, Steve Nash, who hit six free throws in a row down the stretch to surprise the perennial powerhouse. Santa Clara defeated Arizona 64-61. Unfortunately, the team's glory was short-lived, as they bowed out of the tournament in the next round against Temple University. At the end of his freshman year, Nash and his performance on the national stage successfully put Santa Clara on the map for college basketball.

Nash returned to Santa Clara as a sophomore in 1993-1994 amidst high expectations, with the eyes of everyone back home watching. Steve had experienced a successful freshman year and spent the summer spent playing hoops for British Columbia and Canada, earning a silver medal in the World University Games. In his sophomore year, Steve average 14.6 points, 3.7 assists, and 2.5 rebounds per game during the season. Unfortunately, the team did not post a winning record and failed to qualify for the NCAA tournament. Nash had improved since his freshman year, but he was upset by the fact that his team had failed to qualify for the tournament.

Junior Year: A Breakthrough Season

Things changed for the 1994-1995 season. Steve was now on everyone's watch list, receiving attention from the NBA and other top schools. Santa Clara's secret weapon was no longer a secret. During his junior campaign, he topped the conference in three separate categories averaging 20.9 points and 6.4 assists a game, and shooting 45.4 percent from three-point land, earning him a West Coast Conference Player of the Year award. Despite Steve's league-leading efforts, his team was defeated by Mississippi State in the NCAA tournament, 75-67, ending another big season of his college career. After that heartbreaking loss, the question on the minds of everyone in the basketball world was whether or not the basketball phenom from Santa Clara would go pro.

Senior Year: On Top of the College Basketball World

After careful thinking, Nash decided he would earn his college degree and he returned to Santa Clara for his senior year. The 1995-1996 season seemed filled with promise, as

Nash's game was still improving and he did not want to be a second-round pick in the NBA draft, where he had been projected as a junior. Between his junior and senior years, Nash spent more time playing with the Canadian team as well as working out with premier NBA talent such as Jason Kidd and Gary Payton. The 1995-1996 Broncos drew nationwide attention with shocking victories over UCLA and Michigan. Steve Nash once again won West Coast Conference Player of the Year honors. The Broncos, however, lost in the first round of the conference tournament to Pepperdine University.

Fortunately, the Santa Clara Broncos still received an at-large bid to the NCAA tournament. Drawing Maryland as their first round opponent was a tall task for any team that year, but the Broncos were on a mission to make the college basketball world theirs. Led by Nash, who was credited as being the most complete player in all of college basketball at the time, the Broncos beat Maryland 91-79 behind Nash's 28 points and 12 assists. In the next game, they faced one of college basketball's all-time great programs, Kansas, and fell 76-51. Nash faulted himself for the team's loss, citing his poor play; he went only 1 for 11 from the field.

Nash completed his college career after four years, earning a Bachelor of Science in Sociology. Nash was a prolific player for the Santa Clara program, having recorded 510 career assists, going 263 for 656 in three-pointers, scoring 1689 points and hitting 86.2 percent of his free throws. In September of 2006, Santa Clara retired Nash's jersey number 11, cementing his legacy at Santa Clara University.

Next stop: the NBA.

Chapter 4: Steve's NBA Career

The 1996 NBA Draft

The 1996 NBA Draft was a class full of talent. At first glance, nobody thought that the draft class would have so many talented players who would go down in NBA history. After all, nobody can really assess a players' potential until they actually see them develop. Nevertheless, the class of 1996 had names such as Allen Iverson, Stephon Marbury, Ray Allen, Kobe Bryant, Peja Stojakovic, and Ben Wallace. All of those players have become All-Stars and a few of them have won NBA championships. That class would probably go down in history as one of the best classes the NBA has ever seen. But one of the members of that draft class would go down to win more MVP awards than any of the guys mentioned above. Of course, that man is Steve Nash.

Steve Nash was never as heralded in a draft class full of talented guards such as Iverson, Marbury, Allen, and Bryant. Allen Iverson was the consensus top overall pick of the draft because of his stellar college career and because of his natural ability to score despite his size. Nash did not have the quickness and the scoring pedigree of Iverson. He also was not as young and as full of potential as Kobe Bryant was. He was just a skinny white Canadian who played four years of college in a program not known for developing basketball talent.

Standing at nearly 6'3", Nash was entering the draft as a point guard with good height. He was scrawny and unathletic but he was a true point guard in every sense of that phrase. Though not as quick as Iverson or as athletic as Bryant, he was deceptively fast with the ball and used that skill to penetrate and get the ball moving. Steve Nash had good handles coming into the draft and had a good shooting stroke. Nash's ability to shoot the ball could reach as far as the NBA three-pointer and that was the best part of his offensive skill set.

But the best part of Nash's game was his ability as a natural playmaker. His passing skills were so effective that he could easily get assists in college despite mediocre teammates. What was impressive about Nash, aside from his passing, was his very high basketball IQ. It seemed as if he understood the game at a level far above point guards his age. He saw every part of the floor so well that one might think he had two more pairs of eyes around his head. Moreover, he had a very high work ethic, which probably stems from his family's sporting background. Nash's court vision and his natural feel for basketball made him one of the best, if not the best, natural point guards in the 1996 NBA Draft class.[i]

However, one thing that was always missing from Steve Nash's game was his defense. He found it very difficult to stay on his assignment man-to-man despite playing against talent which was not the cream of the crop in college. His average athletic ability makes him not as quick as point guards in the NBA level and it could very well hinder him from being able to defend NBA guards. His ability to create shots was also something he needed to work on, as he could never really get good shots off the dribble.[ii]

Aside from his lack of lack of defense, Nash was a scrawny guy even for his age at that time of 22 years old. Some younger prospects were bigger than he was and his lack of strength would become a defensive liability against bigger guards in the NBA level.

At best, scouts believed Nash develop into a player similar to John Stockton. However, his lack of quickness and hand speed might hinder him from fully reaching Stockton's level. With that, Steve Nash was slated as a possible late first-round draft pick but could also possibly become the best pure point guard in the draft.[iii]

As the NBA Draft got going, the Philadelphia 76ers drafted Allen Iverson as the first guard from the class. The next guard drafted was Stephon Marbury, who was traded to Minnesota for the third guard drafted, Ray Allen. Next was Kerry Kittles as the eight overall pick. The next teams all chose big men until the 13th round. In what was the biggest steal of the 1996 draft, the Lakers traded for the 13th overall pick, Kobe Bryant. Two picks later, the Phoenix Suns, who already had excellent point guards, chose to draft the 6'3" Canadian out of Santa Clara, Steve Nash. Upset with how their team chose another point guard, Suns fans booed Steve Nash as he went up the stage to shake the hand of NBA Commissioner David Stern.

However, those fans would soon bite their tongues as Nash became one of the best point guards in NBA history.

The Rookie Campaign

When originally drafted by the Suns, Nash was drafted with the intention of serving as the backup point guard for All-Star point guard Kevin Johnson. He was also slated to play alongside former MVP Charles Barkley. The plan was to let the young rookie guard learn the ropes of the NBA under the tutelage of the veteran and eventually take over the reins at the point guard position. Steve Nash was supposed to be part of a long-term project at the point guard position in order to give the Suns young leadership at that playmaker role as they were heading towards a rebuilding period.

However, things did not pan out as planned. Prior to the beginning of the 1996 season, the Suns traded perennial All-Star Charles Barkley to the Houston Rockets in for a package that included guys like Sam Cassell, Robert Horry, and two other role players. Sam Cassell, being the more experienced player and a former NBA champion, got more minutes than Nash did. One of Steve's notable games was in the month of November, where he scored 17 points and had 12 assists to record his first career double-double. But he never got the playing time he needed in order to strut his capabilities as a playmaker.

In December of 1996, the Phoenix Suns acquired All-Star point guard Jason Kidd in a trade that was centered around their offseason acquisition, Sam Cassell. Playing behind the likes of Jason Kidd and, for a certain time period at the start of the season, Sam Cassell, there was not much room for a young Steve Nash to get much time on the floor, causing him to spend much of his rookie season on the bench. Despite being the 15th pick in that year's draft, Steve Nash was given limited playing time, averaging 10.5 minutes a game. He was never able to get the time or the platform he needed to get his groove going. During his rookie year, Nash averaged a meager 3.3 points and just 2.1 assists per game.

Second Year, Same Role

Jason Kidd became the Phoenix Suns' full-time starting point guard coming into the 1997-98 season. Their former star playmaker, Kevin Johnson, was already aging and was deteriorating due to injuries. With that, Steve Nash suddenly became the first point guard off the bench after being a third stringer in his first season. New head coach Danny Ainge was also interested in what Steve Nash could do as a point guard. Jason Kidd was undoubtedly their best playmaker that season as he fed capable scorers Rex Chapman, Antonio McDyess, Clifford Robinson, and Danny Manning. But even with Kidd resting on the bench for certain time periods, Ainge still had a capable point guard feeding teammates with assists.

Steve Nash was so capable as a sophomore player that his minutes doubled over his rookie season. He would often play alongside Kidd to give the Suns two point guards on the floor who could both make plays for other players. Despite Nash playing shooting guard in those stretches, he was still effective as he shot very well from the three-point line at 41.5%, which was ranked 13th overall that year in the whole league. He made at least one three-pointer per game that season. The Suns would even play three point guards at the same time with Kidd, Nash, and Johnson all on the floor. Playing alongside two All-Star playmakers, Steve Nash became one of the most improved players in the league and was headed to eventually become a starting point guard.

With their three point guards feeding good scorers, the Suns improved to a 56-26 win-loss record that season. In his second year in the NBA, Steve Nash's per-game averages improved to 9.1 points on 46% shooting, and 3.4 assists. He played 21.9 minutes that year. However, the Suns lost some of their scorers due to injury that season and they were manhandled by the San Antonio Spurs in the playoffs. Despite the disappointing playoff exit, the Suns were happy with how Steve Nash developed into a rising point guard. Nash would credit his improvement to the experience of playing with Kidd and Johnson, who both pushed him hard during practices and gave him helpful insights as NBA veterans.

Trade to the Dallas Mavericks

After only two seasons with the Phoenix Suns, Nash had played very limited minutes, especially during his rookie campaign. He did, however, show that he was indeed a capable point guard in his sophomore year. People began to look at the Suns as a possible contender in the next few years because of their two point guards. However, Nash was rising so fast that he also got the attention of Dallas Mavericks' assistant coach Donnie Nelson, the son of coaching legend Don Nelson. Donnie and Nash had known each other ever since the latter was in Santa Clara. It was also Donnie who convinced the Suns to draft Nash when the former was still working for the Phoenix-based basketball team. He was always impressed by the Santa Clara product and wanted him to go to Dallas.

With Donnie Nelson convincing his father, the head coach of the Mavericks, Don Nelson, that Nash was someone worth building on, the rising point guard was traded to the Dallas Mavericks prior to his third season in the NBA after the 1998 NBA Draft for a package that included three unheralded draftees. It was during his time with the Dallas

Mavericks that Nash developed into one of the top point guards in the league. Playing with talented players such as a young Dirk Nowitzki and Michael Finley, Steve Nash became part of a core group of players that changed the course of a game.

The Mavericks were headed towards a long-term building process especially with their core of young players. The 25-year old scoring wingman Michael Finley was entering the prime of his career and was putting up 20 points a night. Steve Nash, in his third year in the league, became a full-time starter for the Mavericks and started all of the 40 games he played in during the lockout-shortened 1998-99 NBA season. But their most promising player was 20-year old German rookie Dirk Nowitzki, who played most of his rookie season off the bench.

Nash initially struggled as the starting point guard for the Dallas Mavericks, as he was playing with injuries for a few games. Most of all, the Mavericks were still a developing team and had few offensive weapons who could take the pressure off the ball-handlers. Because of that, Steve Nash had arguably the worst offensive season in his NBA career.

He averaged 7.9 points on a poor 36% from the field. He also had his worst three-point percentage at only 37.4%. However, Nash's assists numbers jumped to 5.5 per game and was his career best at that early part of his life as an NBA player. The Mavericks won only 19 games that year but their future was bright with Nash at the helm feeding the likes of Michael Finley and a rising Dirk Nowitzki.

Rising with Dallas

Despite an awful season in his first year with the Dallas Mavericks, Nash was an integral part of the team's improvement. The Mavs made no major offseason moves prior to the 1999-2000 NBA season other than signing Dallas native Dennis Rodman, who was in the twilight of his career. The old NBA champion was considered a distraction for the team and played only 12 games before being waived by the Mavs. He averaged an amazing 14 rebounds for the Mavs despite being "unmotivated".

For Nash's part, he was quickly becoming more integrated into Don Nelson's style of play and was beginning to get the hang of being the top playmaker for his team. But, in the middle of the season, Steve Nash suffered an ankle injury that forced him to miss 25 games. He came back in the season's last month but lost his starting job to veterans Robert Pack and Hubert Davis. Despite the setback, Steve Nash would still show that he was the best point guard on the team, as he recorded several double-digit assist games in March.

While the Dallas Mavericks could not make the playoffs that season with a 40-42 win-loss record, they were more than happy with how the team improved from the previous seasons. It was their first 40-win season in ten years and it was because of their core players. Finley was still scoring more than 20 per game. Cedric Ceballos was scoring as if he was back to his All-Star form. And Nash, despite missing a bunch of games, was getting the hang of the system and was averaging 4.6 assists and 8.6 points on a then career-best 47.7% shooting. Best of all, the team was rising because of Dirk Nowitzki who was developing into a very promising power forward. Dirk averaged 17.5 points and 6.5 rebounds, as he was showcasing his shooting prowess and his ability to score in bunches.

The new millennium marked the full emergence of Steve Nash and the Mavericks. The team was suddenly sold to billionaire Mark Cuban and was quickly becoming a popular team thanks to their enthusiastic owner. Cuban would go on to become one of the more active owners in the whole league and he was also an important piece of the rise of the Mavs. Thanks to the enthusiasm of team ownership, in the 2000-2001 NBA season, Nash evolved into an integral part of the Dallas Mavericks and was arguably their second best player behind Dirk Nowitzki. His fifth season would also become his breakout year as a player.

The team still relied on their core offensive trio of Nowitzki, Nash, and Finley. Dirk became a solid 20-point scorer and was becoming a rising game-changer for the NBA because of his ability to stretch the floor with his shooting. Finley was still a solid scorer but was relegated to being a second option behind Dirk. Best of all, Steve Nash was one of the most improved players in the NBA, averaging 15.6 points and 7.3 assists a game. He was shooting the ball more but his shooting percentages were also rising. Nash established a new career field goal percentage of 48.7% as well as a career high 89.5% from the free throw line.

For the first time in over a decade, Dallas clinched a playoff berth thanks to the improvement of their trio and to midseason acquisition Juwan Howard, a veteran big man. Their 53-29 win-loss record was good enough for the fifth seed in the Western Conference. They were set to go against perennial Western powerhouse, the Utah Jazz, led by 38-year olds Karl Malone and John Stockton. The Jazz were the more experienced team, as their core duo were perennial NBA championship contenders. However, Malone and Stockton, despite playing at amazing levels for their age, were going up against their younger and fresher counterparts, Dirk Nowitzki and Steve Nash. Two of the best players at their respective positions went up against two counterparts who were also to become two of the best.

In their first playoff series in 11 years, the Dallas Mavericks showed that their fresher and younger legs could topple the veteran experience of Malone and Stockton. Not having home-court advantage, the Mavs lost the first two games to the Jazz. However, they went on to win the next three, fueled by their two home-game victories. After toppling the Utah Jazz in Game 5, the Mavs were headed to the second round and it was a valuable experience for the duo of Nash and Nowitzki to triumph over the duo of Stockton and Malone. However, the Dallas Mavericks were manhandled by the better San Antonio Spurs in the Western Conference Semifinals. The Mavs could only muster enough to win a single game, as San Antonio went on to win the series 4-1. Losing in the second round of the playoffs was a bummer for the Mavs but it provided a lot of experience for the growing core of the Dallas Mavericks.

Becoming an All-Star

The 2001-02 season brought new changes to the Dallas Mavericks. From the green cowboy hat, the Mavs changed their logo to the better accepted blue cowboy that they still use. Moreover, the team was rising in popularity and was selling out games more than they used to because of the rising games of Steve Nash and Dirk Nowitzki. The duo brought new life to Dallas and everyone was buying into the high-octane offense infused by Nash's passing prowess and Dirk's scoring capabilities.

The 2001-02 seasons saw Steve Nash earning his first All-Star team selection and All-NBA Third Team honor. He averaged then career bests in scoring and in passing. He assisted on 7.7 baskets per game and scored 17.9 points a night on 48.3% shooting and 45.5% from three-point territory. Dirk Nowitzki was also an All-Star for the first time in his career that season, averaging 20+ points and almost 10 rebounds per game. With their All-Star duo leading the charge, the Mavs were able to get a 57-25 win-loss record and a ticket to the playoffs with home-court advantage in the second round.

The Dallas Mavericks easily took care of a Kevin Garnett-led Minnesota Timberwolves squad in the first round. It was a battle of two of the best young power forwards in the game as Nowitzki was up against Garnett. However, nobody could match up well with Steve Nash. The Mavs ended up sweeping the Wolves in the best-of-five series and none of the games, except for the 7-point Game 1 victory, seemed close. However, they were set to go up against the Sacramento Kings in the second round. The Kings had the best regular season record in the NBA and were also playing the same fast-paced style that the Mavs were, but at a better rate. In the end, the Mavs could only muster up one win. After stealing Game 2 away from the Kings, the Mavs lost three straight and their playoff appearance was once again ended in the second round. Despite the setback, the Mavs were still optimistic about their future, especially with their two best players now being established stars in the NBA.

With a solid cast of role players and veterans surrounding Steve Nash, Dirk Nowitzki, and Michael Finley, the Dallas Mavericks broke through the plateau they set the previous season and were becoming one of the best teams in the NBA. They started the season with 14 straight victories, which was one win shy of tying the record set by the Houston Rockets in 1993. Their strong start to the season was all because of the chemistry between Nash and Nowitzki, who both played to their usual All-Star forms.

Nash repeated his feats of the previous season in 2002-03, getting selected to the All-Star team and being named to the All-NBA Third Team. He averaged 17.7 points and 7.3 assists while playing all 82 games. Dirk Nowitzki also had one of the best seasons in his career as he scored more than 25 points per game. Because of the strong play of that duo, the Mavs 60 games and were the third seed in the ultra-competitive Western Conference.

The Mavericks went up against the Portland Trailblazers in the first round of the playoffs. Even after winning the first three games of the series, the Blazers gave the Mavs a fight and almost got a monumental upset when they were able to force a deciding Game 7. However, the Mavs pulled through and beat Portland in seven games as they were on their way to the second round.

The Dallas Mavericks went on to face their tormentors from the previous post-season, the Sacramento Kings. The Kings brought the fight to the Mavs in the opening game but the latter team got revenge in Game 2 as they blew the Kings out of Sacramento to steal home-court advantage. The Mavs won a double overtime thriller in Dallas but lost two of the next three games to go into another seventh and deciding game. But the Mavericks were just the better team in that playoff series as they fired from all cylinders in a blowout victory in Game 7. With that victory, Nash and Nowitzki were now past the second round for the first time in their careers and were headed for a chance at an NBA Finals appearance.

It was going to be a matchup of the ages in the Western Conference Finals, as the Mavs faced the San Antonio Spurs for a chance to represent the West at the NBA Finals. The Mavericks stole Game 1 away from the Spurs and were looking as if they would give the Spurs a run for their money. The Spurs took Game 2 to tie the series. But tragedy quickly struck the Mavs in Game 3 when their best player, Dirk Nowitzki, went down with a knee injury that sidelined him for the rest of the series. The scoring load left by Dirk befell upon Nash and Finley. Despite a valiant effort to win one more game for Dallas, the Mavericks just could not stop the Spurs without their big German. In the end, the San Antonio Spurs closed out the Mavs in six games and would eventually become the NBA champions that year.

Slow Breakup

After a disappointing Western Conference Finals loss the previous season, the Dallas Mavericks were intent on making the team better for the 2003-04 season by bolstering the lineup with offseason trades. The team acquired high-scoring forward Antawn Jamison and two other role players in exchange for Nick Van Exel and Avery Johnson. They then acquired Antoine Walker in a trade that included Raef LaFrentz and Chris Mills. With two scoring forwards added in the lineup, the Dallas Mavericks had a potent roster filled with offensive options for Nash to choose passing the ball to.

With Walker playing the power forward, Dirk Nowitzki was relegated to playing the center position full-time for the first and only time in his NBA career. Despite playing his usual stellar self, it was evident that there were chemistry issues as a result of the additions. Jamison and Walker were scoring at high paces but they did not gel well with the system and were taking shots away from Nash, Dirk, and Finley. As a result, Nash only scored 14.5 points per game that season; he never really needed to score as much because of the added scoring options. His assists numbers jumped up to 8.8 per game but he was not selected to the All-Star game despite his increased assists and increased free throw percentage.

The Dallas Mavericks would go on to win 52 games out of 82—an eight-game downgrade from the previous season. That was still good enough for the fifth seed in the Western Conference, but it was evident that they did not have the fire they had had the previous season. The Sacramento Kings handily defeated them in only five games as they did not have the chemistry and the intensity they had when they reached the Western Conference Finals in 2003.

After the 2003-2004 NBA season, Steve Nash became a free agent. While Nash wanted to stay in Dallas to continue building with the team and place he had grown to call home for the past six years, Dallas Mavericks owner Mark Cuban was not willing to pay him for a long-term contract for Nash since he was already spending a substantial amount of the NBA salary cap on his other talented players, such as Dirk Nowitzki, Antoine Walker, and Michael Finley.

Cuban offered the two-time All-Star point guard only as much as $9 million dollars for five years and that was too little for a player of Nash's caliber. The Phoenix Suns approached Nash with a six-year, $63 million contract; Nash asked Cuban if he would match, and Cuban declined, leaving Steve to decide it was time to part ways with the Mavericks and he was on his way to the team that drafted him but traded him away. The prodigal son was back in Phoenix after becoming an All-Star in Dallas.

The Return to Phoenix – The MVP Year

The Phoenix Suns in 2004 had undergone quite a bit of transition in the past year. They had shipped off Stephon Marbury and a declining Penny Hardaway to the New York Knicks during the 2003-04 season and had won just 29 games. Amar'e Stoudemire was a young, rising big man who had won the Rookie of the Year two years earlier, Shawn Marion was a force off the dribble, Joe Johnson was a rising scoring option at the perimeter, and the Suns had some wings with potential in Leandro Barbosa and Quentin Richardson. Best of all, they had an ultra offensive-minded coach, Mike D'Antoni, leading the charge from the bench. Sports analysts predicted that Nash's arrival would bring the Suns back to the playoffs as a seventh or eighth seed and an early first-round playoff exit, but nothing more. Steve Nash had never shown any signs that he could lead a team to a high seed in his first eight seasons in the league, they argued. Why should he be expected to do so now?

While Nash was a NBA veteran by 2004 and was already 30 years old, which is like 50 in NBA years, this was the first time he had been asked to lead a team. He had been stuck on the bench in his first stint with the Suns. As a Dallas Maverick, Nash developed into an All-Star and All-NBA player, but Dirk Nowitzki always overshadowed him. Now there was no Dirk and Nash was free to lead the Suns as far as he could, especially since the Suns did not have a reliable veteran leader in the lineup.

The result was an offensive explosion unparalleled by any team in NBA history. Phoenix quickly became a team feared in the transition game. With athletes like Marion and Stoudemire running down the court and sharp passing by Nash, the Suns scored in transition before the opponent's defense could prepare. And if they could not score from the inside in transition, they had the likes of Joe Johnson and Quentin Richardson ready to catch and shoot from three in transition.

The fast-paced offense quickly drew fans excited to see lots of scoring, but what many people missed was that Phoenix's half-court offense was also incredibly deadly. Nash routinely would use his great handles and coordination to drive past defenders and get into the paint. Either the opposing big man guarding the paint could stand back and let Nash shoot his amazing jumper, or they could come out to defend against Nash. If they came out, Nash could either drive past them and score the layup or pass the ball for the assist. Phoenix leapt from scoring less than 95 points a game in 2003-04 to scoring more than 110 points a game in 2004-05. It was all thanks to Steve Nash directing the offense and dictating the tempo.

How had the Suns become so good? Some pointed to Stoudemire's development. Others credited Mike D'Antoni. But, as the season wore on, it became clear that Nash was the catalyst behind Phoenix's sudden rejuvenation. Nash became a leader—something he didn't get a chance to be in his first stint with Phoenix and in his six seasons with the Mavs. He became the fuel for a high-octane, fast-paced offense that fed off of his amazing passes and his ability to dictate the tempo.

The Suns won 62 games in 2004-05 and had the best record in the NBA. With just the addition of Steve Nash, the Suns won 33 more games compared to the year before. Nash's importance to the Suns was further emphasized by the fact that, in the seven games Nash missed that season with injury, Phoenix only went 2-5. Overall, Nash averaged 15.5 points and led the league with 11.5 assists per game. In 2005, Nash made the All-Star team for the third time as well as the All-NBA First Team for the first time in his career. He became a legitimate superstar in the NBA even after not being an All-Star or even an All-NBA selection the previous season. But in one of the most controversial award choices in NBA history, Steve Nash received the MVP award for the 2004-05 season.

The problem with Nash's MVP award, as opponents argued both then and today, was that Nash was not the only player who had revitalized a NBA franchise that season. Hall of Fame center and multiple-time NBA champion Shaquille O'Neal had been traded from the Los Angeles Lakers to the Miami Heat before the 2004-05 season began. Without O'Neal, the Lakers won just 34 games in 2005 after winning 57 in 2004. With O'Neal, Miami won 59 games in 2005 after winning 42 in 2004. Furthermore, as brilliant as Nash was that season, he was still understood to be a defensive liability. Shaq was good on both defense and offense, so why should the award go to Nash instead?

The voting for the MVP award was incredibly close. Nash prevailed over Shaq 1066-1032 and had 65 first-place votes to Shaq's 58. Despite the arguments in favor of Shaq, he was derailed by the fact that a rising Miami guard named Dwayne Wade also had an excellent season of his own. Some analysts wondered if Wade's development was a bigger reason for Miami's turnaround instead of O'Neal's arrival. But some would even go to argue that Amar'e Stoudemire, who led the Suns in scoring with 26 points per game, was an even bigger factor for the rise of the Phoenix Suns from obscurity. Whatever the discussion around Shaq, Nash was still a reasonable choice thanks to Phoenix's turnaround and how much their offense had improved. But while Phoenix's high-paced offense had led the Suns to many wins, how well could it function in the playoffs?

In the first round of the playoffs, the Suns faced the Memphis Grizzlies and swept them in four games. Some would argue that the sweep was because the Grizzlies didn't have enough experience in the postseason to even get a win. The Suns then took on Nash's old team, the Dallas Mavericks. The Mavericks had revamped themselves a great deal since Nash's departure. They had used the money they saved by letting Nash go to sign center Erick Dampier. Dallas also let Coach Don Nelson go and replaced him with a more conventional coach in Avery Johnson, who used to play with Dallas but was traded away for Jamison. With Dampier and Johnson, Dallas's defense had massively improved. Despite losing Nash, Dallas's record had actually improved from 52 to 58 wins over the past season due to their improved defense. How well would Nash do against his former teammates?

Would he wilt during the playoffs under the pressure of being the MVP?

Nash did not wilt and instead tore the Mavericks to shreds. In Game 3, Nash had 27 points and 17 assists in the Phoenix victory. He then scored 48 points in Game 4, though that was marred by 9 turnovers that contributed to Phoenix's defeat. But it was Game 6 in Dallas that showed that Nash was capable of coming through when his team needed him most. Dallas made big runs throughout the game, leading by double digits late in the third quarter.

Whenever the game seemed about to slip out of hand, Nash was there. With less than ten seconds left in regulation, Nash hit a huge three-pointer to tie the game at 111 and to send it into overtime. During the overtime period, Nash had 7 points and 2 assists to clinch Phoenix's victory and their first trip to the Western Conference Finals since 1993. He finished with 39 points, 12 assists, and 9 rebounds. In the series against Dallas, Nash averaged a ridiculous 30.3 points on 55% shooting, 12 assists, and 6.5 rebounds. He had missed just one free throw through all six games. It might have been a product of Nash's great improvement but some could say that revenge was in his mind when he played his best against the team that did not see him as nothing more than a $9 million player.

Unfortunately, that was the end of the road for the Phoenix Suns. They faced the San Antonio Spurs, led by dominant power forward Tim Duncan and their tough defense. The Suns also missed their starting shooting guard Joe Johnson due to injury for their first two games. Nash played his heart out and averaged 23 points and 11 assists for the series. But without Johnson, Nash lacked a potent scoring option to pass to in the wings and Phoenix's perimeter defense could not contain Spurs shooting guard Manu Ginobili and San Antonio prevailed in 5 games. The Phoenix Suns may have won many regular season games, but was it possible that their system was just a fluke or a gimmick? Many people thought so and it led many to think that their offensive style was just not fit for the intensity of the playoffs.

Second MVP Season

Coming back for the 2005-06 season Nash proved to his doubters that he was no gimmick. During the 2005 offseason, Joe Johnson left to sign with the Atlanta Hawks. Then right before the 2005-06 season began, Stoudemire was forced to undergo micro-fracture surgery, a major knee operation that requires months to recover. He ended up missing the entire season. Faced without Amar'e or Johnson, two of his best options to pass to, Nash responded with arguably the best season of his career.

The Suns still played with the same kind of high-octane offense that made them a serious title contender the previous season. Nash and D'Antoni proved that their style of play was not simply a product of the great offensive players they had because a lot of the other role players stepped up in order to fill the gap left by Stoudemire and Johnson. Shooting guard Raja Bell, who was merely a shooter and defensive option on his previous teams, came into the Suns and filled the huge gap left by Johnson. He had the best season of his career as he scored 14.7 points a game and shot his career best 45.7% from the floor and

44% from three-point land. From being a shooting guard with Atlanta, Boris Diaw became the starting center for the Suns as he upgraded three positions up. Though he did not have the dominance of Stoudemire, he did fill in nicely as he improved his numbers from merely 4 points with the Hawks to 13 per game for the Suns. Lastly, Leandro Barbosa was becoming a potent option of the bench as quick as his feet could move.

Even though they no longer had a great big man like Stoudemire who could finish Nash's passes, the Suns still remained one of the best offenses in the league. Nash averaged 18.8 points and 10.5 assists per game. He also joined the 50-40-90 club for the first time in his career as he shot 51.2% from the floor, 43.9% from three, and 92.1% from the foul line. But the Suns struggled even more when, in late February, defensive specialist Kurt Thomas was also ruled out for the season with injury. For the rest of the season, Phoenix would rely on the 6'8'' Boris Diaw to play at the center position. Despite these difficulties, Phoenix still won 54 games and clinched the second seed in the Western Conference. Nash showed the world that his first

MVP season was not a fluke. Best of all, he showed that unselfish passing can turn a team of role players into serious title contenders.

It was an impressive accomplishment by Nash, and he earned his second straight MVP that year. There was no controversy that year regarding his MVP season because nobody was even close to him in the voting, as no other player meant so much to his team to get some consideration for the award. The closest in the voting was 21-year old phenom LeBron James, who tallied 688 voting points against Nash's 983. Nevertheless, a lot of people still believed that he did not deserve that second MVP, especially since Kobe Bryant tore up the league with 35 points per game that season, including an 81-point performance. In any case, Steve Nash was that season's MVP and all the voters knew that he was the most deserving for that award. Not a lot of point guards in NBA history can claim to have been an MVP much less a back-to-back winner for that award.

In the playoffs, the Suns made another deep run to the Western Conference Finals. First off, they went up against the Los Angeles Lakers, led by Kobe Bryant, who was on a scoring rampage that season. After winning Game 1 at home, the Suns went on to lose the next three games. The Lakers capped off their three-game win streak with an overtime win in Game 4 as Bryant sank a game-winning jump shot over two defenders. However, the Suns regain their form and beat the Lakers three straight in dominant fashion to get rid of the pesky seventh-seeded team.

Up next, the Suns faced off against another Los Angeles team. This time, it was the Clippers. Though the Clippers were historically a bad team, they gave as much of a fight to the Phoenix Suns as the Lakers did. On the strength of Nash's 30 points and 12 assists, the Suns managed to survive a 40-point explosion by Elton Brand. They split the next four games, capped off by a double overtime win by the Suns in Game 5. The Clippers managed to force Game 7 with a 12-point win in Game 6. But in the clinching game of the series, the Suns returned to form and they fended off the gritty Clippers with a 20-point victory, as Marion led the way with 30 points and Nash assisted on 11 baskets.

Steve Nash, for the second straight year, would go on to face his old team in the playoffs. This time, the Mavericks were improved from the previous year, as they were a more potent team with guys like Jason Terry and Josh Howard helping Dirk Nowitzki in scoring. Nash would have loved to eliminate his old team for the second straight season. However, it was then and there when he realized that they needed Stoudemire more than ever. Nobody in the Suns' lineup could equal the output of Dirk through the whole series. Though Phoenix won Game 1, the Mavs went on to win two straight. In Game 5, Dirk scored 50 big points and the disheartened Suns could not force a Game 7, as they lost to the Mavs in six games.

Continued Reign as the Best Point Guard in the NBA

While Phoenix had failed to reach the NBA Finals past two years, 2006-07 was supposed to be the season when they finally succeeded. Stoudemire was fully recovered and did not miss a single game. He and Nash formed a devastating offensive pairing on the pick and roll, and the rest of the Suns worked around them to slash, pass, or shoot.

With their full strength back in action, Nash was finally able to see again what it was like to have better options to pass to. While Stoudemire was back to lead the team in scoring, several other players either stepped up or remained consistent. Shawn Marion remained as a potent scorer and terrific undersized rebounder. Raja Bell was scoring and shooting as well as he did the previous season. Best of all, Leandro Barbosa became the best bench scorer in the league and was named the Sixth Man of the Year. Everyone was clicking for the Suns as they remained the highest scoring team for the third straight year. By some advanced metrics, the 2006-07 Suns are the greatest offensive team of all time and they ranked tops in field goal percentage and three-point percentage that year. Again, it was all thanks to world's best point guard Steve Nash leading the team with his passing abilities.

The Suns won 61 games in the 2006-07 season, second in the NBA behind the Dallas Mavericks. Nash made the All-Star Team and All-NBA First Team again. Even though voters were uneasy about giving Nash a third straight MVP, he still placed second in voting behind Dirk

Nowitzki. It was one of the closest MVP votes in the history of the NBA. Dirk wound up with a total of 1138 points, while Nash had 1013. The first-place votes were key: Dirk got 83 while the superstar point guard had 44. But if you would ask any expert, had Nash won the MVP that season, it would have been the most deserving of his MVP awards because he was the main catalyst for the Suns' emergence the past three seasons.

As the 2007 NBA playoffs began, Dirk's Mavericks were the favorites to win the NBA title. But, when Dallas was shockingly upset by the Golden State Warriors in the first round, it appeared that Phoenix's time had come. The Suns were up to face the Lakers for the second straight year. This time, the Phoenix Suns were better than they were in 2006 and the Lakers would have no chance to win the series. Just a year after winning their first round series in seven games, the Suns handily defeated the Lakers in five.

After beating the Los Angeles Lakers in the first round, they faced the San Antonio Spurs in the second round. If Phoenix could beat the Spurs, the championship would be theirs for the taking. The Spurs and the Suns fought incredibly hard and evenly split the first four games of the series. Three of the games were close and decided by less than ten points. However, the rest of the series was marred by a single play during the final seconds of Game 4. With 20 seconds left in the game, Phoenix had all but secured the win. After the Spurs missed a shot, Nash secured the rebound and rushed the ball up the court. Spurs forward Robert Horry delivered a hard check on Nash, who slammed hard into the scoring table. A scuffle between the two teams broke out. But while the fight was quickly broken up and the Suns won the game, an irate Amar'e Stoudemire and Boris Diaw had left the bench to check on their teammate. Under NBA rules, if a player in the bench area walks onto the court during a fight, he is automatically suspended for one game. The NBA promptly suspended Stoudemire and Diaw, and the Suns lost the next two games and the series. While it is impossible to know for certain, one can speculate that the suspension and Robert Horry's cheap shot might have cost Phoenix the series and their chances for a championship. The Spurs would go on to become the NBA champions that year after sweeping the Cleveland Cavaliers in the Finals.

The following years were also successful for Nash but, as a team, Phoenix faced a competitive landscape in the Western Conference. During the course of the next season, Nash continued to dissect opposing defenses as the NBA's best playmaker. Nash's quick speed with and away from the ball gave Phoenix a man who could take over a game when needed. Nash possessed an ability to finish at the basket or pull up and drain a three-pointer. Adding his ability to push a quick outlet pass or dump the ball in the lane, Nash was a legitimate triple threat. With Nash running the point and a talented surrounding cast, Phoenix was consistently one of the highest scoring offenses in the league, moving and shooting the ball quickly.

The 2007-08 season was arguably the most competitive season the West has had in recent years. A lot of teams won 50 games that season, including the Phoenix Suns. The Suns kept their core unit intact to start the season and their main offseason acquisition was 35-year old Grant Hill. In Phoenix, Hill would rejuvenate his career. despite being in his twilight years and despite suffering a myriad of injuries over his long career. He credited his longevity to the Suns' training staff, who also did a good job of keeping Nash healthy and in shape despite playing in his deep 30s with Phoenix.

In the middle of the season, the Phoenix Suns decided that their core players could no longer keep them competitive especially as the Western Conference teams were beginning to get bigger frontlines. Hence, the Suns' front office decided to deal Shawn Marion to the Miami Heat in exchange for legendary big man and another player in his twilight years, Shaquille O'Neal. They decided for the trade as Mario was no longer providing the scoring punch he did in previous season and, with Shaq in the lineup, the Suns got a bigger lineup as Stoudemire was relegated to playing the power forward position.

Despite the upgrades to their frontcourt, there were spacing problems with Shaq and Amar'e. As good as they were individually, there was a problem in terms of their role in clogging up the paint offensively. As the Suns were a high-tempo and jump-shooting team, they wanted the floor stretched as far as possible but Shaq and Amar'e were both paint dwellers at that point in their careers. Moreover, Shaq could not run as fast and as well as Marion did and his acquisition effectively ended the run-and-gun style that almost got the Suns an NBA Finals appearance. Luckily, Nash could still feed either of them easily and both players were shooting about 60% throughout the season.

The Phoenix Suns ended the season with a 55-27 record. As they were playing in a very competitive Western Conference, their record was only good enough for the sixth seed. Nash was still an All-Star despite a slight dip in his numbers. He averaged 16.9 points and 11.1 assists per game. He joined the 50-40-90 club for the second time in his career and was an All-NBA Second Team member after three straight seasons of being in the First Team. It was also in that season that another stellar point guard name Chris Paul was beginning to overtake Nash's place as the best point guard in the NBA.

The Suns would once again face the San Antonio Spurs, the defending champions who eliminated them from a possible Finals appearance almost a year before. With Shaq in the lineup, the Suns were able to match up well with Tim Duncan. However, the Spurs were just too well-coached and more experienced than the Suns. The defending NBA champions went on to win three straight games. Though Phoenix staved off a sweep by winning Game 4, it was still futile as the Spurs went on to beat them in five games.

The End of the D'Antoni Era

After their defeat at the hands of San Antonio Spurs once again, Mike D'Antoni left the Phoenix Suns organization to sign with the New York Knicks as its new head coach for the 2008-09 season. Terry Porter replaced D'Antoni as the new head coach of the Phoenix Suns. As Porter preferred a more defensive style of basketball, something the Suns and Nash never really tried playing, the run-and-gun era officially ended for the Suns. In the NBA draft, the Suns were able to acquire young talent in defensive center Robin Lopez and dynamic Slovenian point guard Goran Dragic.

As the Suns were never really used to playing the defensive brand, they struggled throughout the 2008-09 season and they tried to remedy the struggle by trading away Bell and Diaw for scoring wingman Jason Richardson from the Charlotte Bobcats (now Hornets). Despite the trades, the Suns still struggled and this forced the Phoenix front office to fire Terry Porter in the middle of the season without even having the chance to finish a full year as head coach. Porter was succeeded by Alvin Gentry, who was intent on bringing back the up-tempo style that made the Suns relevant.

As the Suns struggled throughout the year to adjust to different head coaching styles, Nash's numbers suffered and it resulted to him not being selected as an All-Star for the first time in his career since coming back to the Phoenix Suns. However, teammate Shaquille O'Neal, who was experiencing a rejuvenated career with the Suns, was selected as an All-Star and was co-MVP in the midseason classic together with Kobe Bryant.

The Suns, despite a late push due to the coaching of Alvin Gentry, were not able to secure the final playoff berth. That was the first time that Nash and the Suns missed the playoffs since the star point guard returned to the organization in 2005. In the 2008-09 season, Steve Nash averaged 15.7 points and 9.7 assists. His assists numbers were the lowest he had had in his second stint with the Suns. He did, however, join the 50-40-90 club for the third time in his career as he shot the ball from the floor at 50%, had a three-point percentage of about 44%, and shot 93.3% from the foul line.

Return to the Western Conference Finals

With Alvin Gentry at the helm, the Suns went back to their strength of playing a running style of basketball. Though their core players from Mike D'Antoni's era were no longer with the team, they still had their best duo of Nash and Stoudemire playing great pick-and-roll basketball. And, with Shaquille O'Neal leaving the team to go to Cleveland, the Suns could go back to play a faster style of basketball.

The Phoenix Suns opened the season strong, as they won 8 of their first 9 games. This was due to Nash playing the style he was always comfortable with. But with Gentry, the attack was balanced instead of relying on a handful of scoring options. Also, the Suns enjoyed more floor spacing as they surrounded their star point guard with shooters. Nash's first option remained Amar'e Stoudemire, who was left free to roam the paint without O'Neal. But if Stoudemire wasn't available, Nash had a bevy of shooters and capable scorers surrounding the perimeter. The team had the likes of Jason Richardson, Grant Hill, Jared Dudley, Channing Frye, and Leandro Barbosa. All of those players contributed night in and night out and they helped the Suns become a Western Conference contender.

Because of the Suns' re-emergence as a powerhouse, their star point guard saw a return to the All-Star game as a starter. He also won the Skills Challenge for the second time in his career. His leadership on the court had the Suns leading the league in scoring for the fifth straight season and he also helped the team return to the playoffs as a third seed. At the end of the 2009-10 regular season, Nash averaged his usual numbers with 16.5 points and 11 assists per game. It was the fourth time in his career that he led the league in assists. He was also back in the 50-40-90 club for the third straight season and solidified himself as one of the most efficient shooters in the history of the NBA, as he became the leader for most 50-40-90 seasons in NBA history. Nash was also selected as a member of the All-NBA Second Team. That would be the final time that Steve Nash was a member of an All-NBA team.

Nash and the Suns were slated to go up against the sixth-seeded Portland Trailblazers. The Suns lost Game 1 on their home court. Nash, although playing well, was outplayed by the opposing point guard Andre Miller, who had 31 points and 8 assists. Nash had 25 and 9 as the Suns barely lost to Portland. They took revenge in Game 2 by blowing the Trailblazers out of Phoenix. Jason Richardson exploded for 29 points and Nash was distributing the ball at a high rate throughout the entire game. He had 16 assists to contribute to the 119-90 win.

In Portland, the Suns regained home-court advantage by winning Game 3. Jason Richardson capped off a solid two-game stretch with a 42-point outburst while Nash had 10 assists. The Blazers bounced back in Game 4   as   the Suns struggled to score. Nash only got 8 assists in that game and their only bright spot was the 26-point performance by Amar'e Stoudemire.

Back in Phoenix for Game 5, role player Channing Frye got his groove going by leading a balanced Suns attack to solidify their series lead. The bench got going in that game and Nash needed to play only 27 minutes for 10 assists. Bench players Frye and Dudley, who had 19, contributed well. Backup point guard Goran Dragic contributed 7 points. In Portland for Game 6, the Trailblazers were thinking of extending the series to Game 7 as they tried to rally a comeback. But the Suns withstood the run and went on to win the game, 99 to 90. Richardson, after a slump, scored 28 points in the closeout game. Nash only had 6 assists.

The Suns went on to face the San Antonio Spurs in the second round. The Spurs had struggled in the regular season and were only able to get the seventh seed in the West as they were unable to play their usual consistent high level of basketball. The Spurs had tormented the Suns for the past five years. If there was a time for Nash to get revenge, 2010 was the best time to do so because the Spurs looked like a shell of their former selves that year.

In Game 1, Nash seemed like a man on a mission. He scored the ball at a pace unseen from a 35-year old point guard. He put up shot after shot and they all went in for the efficient-shooting All-Star. Nash had 33 points and 10 assists and the Spurs just could not stop him from wreaking havoc on the floor. And it wasn't as if he was a one-man show. Richardson also got going with 33 points on an equally efficient shooting night and so did Amar'e Stoudemire, who had 23 points.

Though Nash wasn't able to do an encore of his Game 1 performance, his teammates helped him get the Game 2 win. He had 19 points and 6 assists. Stoudemire had 23 points and Richardson had 19. The bench also contributed, as Frye dialed from long range with 5 three-pointers and Dudley had 11 points. Despite a 29-point output from Big Timmy, the Spurs were down 0-2 to the rejuvenated Phoenix Suns.

In Game 3, Stoudemire was limited to 7 points, while Nash had 16 points and 6 assists. But it was the "other guys" who scored big for the Suns. Former superstar Grant Hill scored 18 points and it seemed like he wasn't an elder statesman in the league. But the story of the game was a Slovenian backup point guard who only played 17 minutes but had 26 points, including 5 of 5 from beyond the three-point line. Dragic's fourth-quarter charge was key for the Suns in getting a 3-0 lead in the series and they were virtually a shoo-in for the Western Conference Finals.

With revenge already in the palm of their hands, the Suns needed only one victory to sweep the Spurs and proceed to the Western Conference Finals for the first time since losing to San Antonio in the 2007 playoffs. Facing a competitive final quarter from the Spurs who were playing desperately to keep their season alive, the Suns went back to their two stars, who combined for 22 points in the fourth quarter. At the end of the game, Stoudemire had 29 points while Nash had 20 points and 9 dimes for the Suns, who swept the Spurs in four games. By defeating the Spurs, Nash exorcised his San Antonio demons and was again playing at a chance for the NBA Finals.

In the way of the Phoenix Suns were the defending champions, the Los Angeles Lakers. The Suns and the Lakers were bitter playoff rivals and the Suns had eliminated the Lakers from the playoffs twice in the past. As the Suns sought revenge from their own playoff tormentors, it was the Lakers' turn to do so and their superstar Kobe Bryant, Nash's draftmate in 1996, was in the mood to do so.

The Suns could not stop the superstar shooting guard from dominating the Suns in Game 1. The Black Mamba scored 40 points and made mincemeat of the Suns' defense. His 40 points were enough to give a 21-point blowout victory for the Lakers. On his part, Nash could not equal that output and had only 13 points and 13 assists.

While the Suns defended Kobe better in Game 2, the Lakers just had too many offensive weapons. Pau Gasol scored 29 points to lead a fourth-quarter rally by the Lakers. The Suns played them to a stalemate for three quarters led by the 27 points of Jason Richardson but they just could not contain the offensive prowess of the defending champions. Nash had his second subpar scoring output with 11 points, but he did have 15 dimes.

The Suns went home to Phoenix to host the Lakers in Game 3. This time, it was their turn to explode. Despite not being able to contain Kobe's 36 points and 11 assists, the Suns defended the other Lakers well. Of course, scoring is the name of the game and nobody did it better than the Suns. Amar'e Stoudemire had 42 big points. Role player Robin Lopez had 20 and Richardson had 19. Nash chose not to score big and only had 17 points. But his 15 assists were key in helping the Suns get the victory.

After once again failing to contain Kobe, who had 36 points in Game 4, the Suns got a lot of help from their bench players in order to tie the series 2-2. The Suns mounted a huge fourth-quarter rally, with their bench players playing big throughout the final 12 minutes. Nash struggled to get his 15 points and had only 8 assists. But they were so deep that the starters did not need to come up big. Frye scored 14 points and had 4 triples. Dudley scored 11 while Barbosa had 14.

Game 5 was an instant classic as the two teams battled each other to a stalemate. Whatever punches the Suns threw, the Lakers would throw counterpunches to equal the

Suns' output. Game 5 was also Steve Nash's best game in the series. He had 29 points and 11 assists. Kobe tried to equal Nash with a near triple-double output of 30 points, 11 rebounds, and 9 assists. Despite the big games by the two superstars, the outcome boiled down to one last play. As the game was in the final few seconds, Kobe Bryant shot a contested three-pointer with the game tied at 101. But it was Ron Artest who fought his way for the offensive rebound and putback to win the game at the buzzer. Artest only had 4 points but his final 2 were the biggest points of the game.

Facing elimination on their own home floor, the Suns had to play their best and had to be desperate in Game 6. After matching a big opening quarter by the Lakers, Phoenix was at the losing end of a Laker rally that stemmed from the second quarter up to the third. Down 17 points entering the fourth quarter, the Suns tried to mount a comeback that could send the series to Game 7. Nash had 21 points and 9 assists and Amar'e had 27 for the game. But it was just too much Kobe Bryant, who scored 37 points. Game 5 hero Ron Artest had 25 points on an efficient 10-of-16 shooting.

In the end, the Suns just got not muster enough strength to beat the defending champs. And if they were going to go back to whatever went wrong, they would see that defense was once again their bane as they could not contain Bryant throughout the whole series.

Without Amar'e, a Rebuilding Stage

Despite a deep playoff run that brought the written-off Suns to the cusp of an NBA Finals appearance, that was the deepest they and Nash could go in recent memory. Knowing that he might not get back to championship contention with the Suns, Amar'e Stoudemire decided not to accept the 5-year, $95 million contract offered by the Suns' organization and went to the New York Knicks instead for a $100 million contract. Amar'e was reunited with Mike D'Antoni, who was the Knicks' head coach then.

Without Nash's best assist option and the team's leading scorer, the organization went to sign veterans instead in an attempt to fill in the void that Stoudemire left and in order to give more options for their aging two-time MVP point guard. They acquired Hedo Turkoglu and Hakim Warrick in order to bolster the bench and make the team competitive. Though Warrick was not the offensive force that Amar'e was, he was athletic enough to finish pick-and-roll plays.

The Suns initially failed to be competitive in the strong Western Conference. Seeing that their offseason acquisitions and their roster could not match up well with other Western powerhouses, they decided to overhaul the squad by trading away Jason Richardson and Turkoglu to the Orlando Magic, who were trying desperately to stay strong in order to retain the services of All-Star center Dwight Howard. The Suns received former superstar Vince Carter, Marcin Gortat, and Mickael Pietrus from the Magic. But the overhaul did not stop there. Before the trade deadline, they moved Goran Dragic to the Houston Rockets in exchange for Aaron Brooks.

With all the movements and additions to the team, Nash stayed his usual stellar self. The former MVP was so experienced as a player that he no longer needed to adjust to his new teammates. Steve Nash was still throwing passes to open players at such a high rate that nobody could have imagined that the star point guard was already 36 years old that year. Despite his advanced age and new teammates, Steve Nash still led the NBA in assists that season and was beating out younger point guards like Rajon Rondo, Chris Paul, and Deron Williams even as he was playing with mediocre teammates on only 33 minutes a night.

However, Nash did not make the All-Star team that season, even though he played younger than his age. It might have been because the Suns struggled to stay above .500. Had they been a playoff contender, Steve Nash would surely have made the All-Star team. In addition to leading the league in assists with 11.4 per game, he scored 14.7 points a night on another efficient shooting season. Nash, however, failed to post a 50-40-90 season as he barely shot 50% from the floor and 40% from three-point territory. The Suns, with a 40-42 win-loss record did not qualify for the playoffs that year and it seemed like Nash's window to win a championship was closing in on the two-time MVP.

Before the 2011-12 season could get going, the league entered a lockout period that ended in December. Because of the lockout, teams and players were stagnant and only had until December to start training camp. The season was also shortened to 66 games. While most other players were either out of shape or not in the rhythm entering the new season, Steve Nash was as fit as ever and had enough time to rest his aging bones in the long offseason break.

The Suns still failed to form a formidable lineup to compete for a playoff spot in the 2011-12 season. Their best offseason move was drafting a versatile 6'10" power forward, Markieff Morris, from out of Kansas. They also signed the athletic guard Shannon Brown whose best years were playing as Kobe Bryant's backup in the Lakers' back-to-back championship seasons. With another mediocre lineup, nobody expected the Suns to be competitive.

Expectations were indeed true. The Suns once again struggled to win more than half of their games and seemed like a shell of their former selves in offense. They dropped down to being the eighth highest scoring team in the NBA after leading the league in scoring for half a decade.

Though the team was filled with role players, Steve Nash got them to stay afloat by making plays for players who otherwise could not create shots for themselves. Steve Nash was proving to the world that his assist numbers were not the product of a run-and-gun system filled with good scorers, because he was still able to rack up the assists even with mediocre teammates.

Nash was still averaging about 11 assists a night as a 37-year old point guard. His best option for passes was a rising center Marcin Gortat, who had been Dwight Howard's backup in Orlando. With Nash making life easy, Gortat was able to up his numbers to about 15 points per game and was the Suns' leading scorer. Despite the improvements, he was not Amar'e Stoudemire on offense and the Suns were still struggling. However, coaches around the league recognized Nash's importance to the Suns and his ability to play at a high level despite his advanced age. He was voted in as an All-Star player as he was leading the league that time in assists. That would be his eighth and last All-Star game appearance in an amazing career worthy of the Hall of Fame.

At the end of the season, the Phoenix Suns once again failed to make the playoffs with a 33-33 win-loss record. Steve Nash failed to become the assists leader, as Rajon Rondo edged him out at the tail end of the season. But he was able to pass Oscar Robertson in the career assists ladder and climbed up to sixth behind Magic Johnson. Nash averaged 12.5 points and 10.7 assists that year. He shot the ball efficiently again but failed to make it into the 50-40-90 club with only 39% shooting from three-point range and 89.4% from the charity stripe.

After the 2011-2012 NBA season, it became clear that Phoenix would have to begin rebuilding as a franchise and that the Steve Nash era might be over. It only seemed fair that the organization, which Nash had spent the last eight years of his career playing for, gave their beloved star an opportunity to pursue what every player in the NBA hopes and dreams of growing up: winning an NBA championship. Though Nash would never publically demand a trade, fans and NBA experts around the league believed that it would only be right if Phoenix gave Steve one last shot at a championship since his window to win one was starting to close at the age of 38.

Leaving Phoenix for Los Angeles

Steve Nash was acquired by the Los Angeles Lakers as part of a sign-and-trade deal prior to the start of the 2012-13 season. Many people thought that bringing in a player like Steve Nash to join a talented team that included Kobe Bryant, Dwight Howard, and Pau Gasol made the Los Angeles Lakers legitimate championship contenders. The Lakers were looking at another possible run at the NBA championship, a feat that Nash had never accomplished in his many years in the NBA. Upon his arrival in Los Angeles, Nash had to switch jersey numbers, since his number 13 was retired in the name of the NBA great Wilt Chamberlain. Fans began to put that Lakers team up on the Western Conference pedestal, especially as they had present and former All-Stars at each of the five starting positions. People smelled a championship ring in Los Angeles and on Nash's finger.

Unfortunately for Nash, the 2012-13 Lakers never managed to reach their potential. Kobe and Howard feuded with one another over who needed to be the top offensive choice and the Lakers never developed the team chemistry needed for a winning team. Coaching was also to blame, as Mike Brown's failure to implement a solid offensive system got him fired early in the season. It was a disastrous start to the season and the Lakers never got their core starting five together on the floor for long stretches because of injuries.

Nash also struggled during the 2012-13 season. At almost 39 years old, it seemed that age and injuries finally caught up with him and he missed 32 games, primarily because of an injury he suffered early in the season. He was supposed to be a core piece to that strong lineup after Mike D'Antoni took over the coaching reigns of the LA Lakers. Nash also only averaged 6.7 assists that year, his lowest output since 1999. However, on January 8, 2013, on an assist to Antawn Jamison, Steve Nash became just the fifth player in NBA history to record 10,000 career assists.

Halfway through the season it was decided that Kobe Bryant would defend the other team's primary ball handler, taking some of the defensive pressure off of Nash. Another important change made around that time was that Bryant became the primary ball handler for the Lakers, changing Nash's offensive role to more of a spot-up shooter. The switch would enable the 17-year veteran to focus on just shooting the ball, since he was having trouble running the team's pick-and-roll offense. But that plan went out the window when Bryant tore his Achilles just two games before the playoffs began. This was a big blow to the Lakers because the team was only beginning to gel and Kobe was on an offensive tear that saw him averaging 27 points as a 34-year old wingman. Despite their early chemistry struggles and the injuries they suffered, the Lakers limped to the playoffs as they became the seventh seed in the West with a record of 45-37. Nash had additional health problems at the end of the season as well, and only played two games in the playoffs. He averaged 12.7 points and 6.7 assists while barely missing the 50-40-90 mark again. He appeared in only 50 games that year.

The LA Lakers squared off with the San Antonio Spurs in the first round of the playoffs. There was just something about Nash that always got him facing the Spurs in the playoffs almost every time. He was like a Spurs magnet. Unfortunately, the being a Spurs magnet meant that the Lakers were in for a tough outing. The Spurs were playing younger than their age and they were very well coached with an offensive system that has worked year in and year out since 1997. And without their best player, Kobe Bryant, the Lakers' best weapon was an unhappy Dwight Howard.

The Spurs immediately ran roughshod over the Lakers as the playoffs started. The Los Angeles-based team seemed as if they did not know what hit them as the Spurs dominated them in Game 1 with a 91-79 win. Game 2 would be no different and the Spurs headed for a 2-0 lead with an 11-point win. The Lakers seemed as if they just could not defend the solid ball movement of the Spurs and they were doomed from the start.

Game 3 in Los Angeles was a lot worse. The Spurs got everyone going while the Lakers had only Howard and

Gasol to rely on. The twin towers were not big enough to make the Lakers competitive and they lost by 31 points. With the Lakers virtually eliminated from the playoffs, Game 4 was merely a formality and the Spurs finally got rid of the disappointing LA Lakers with a 103-82 victory.

With the Lakers losing big to the Spurs in the playoffs, Steve Nash's final chance for an NBA championship seemed all but gone. Kobe was out with an Achilles injury and might not be able to get back to playing at a high level. It seemed that Dwight Howard no longer wanted to stay as a Laker with all the pressure weighing down on him. Metta World Peace, the former Ron Artest, was aging and could no longer defend the best small forwards. Finally, Pau Gasol was still an All-Star caliber player but was unhappy with D'Antoni's system, as he felt that his skills were being underutilized.

Continued Injury Problems

The short-lived Laker powerhouse team was all but over after only one season. Dwight Howard decided to forego his opportunity to stay with the Lakers and went over to the

Houston Rockets to team up with James Harden. Meanwhile, World Peace was waived by the team and Kobe Bryant struggled to get back from his serious injury. Though Nash remained a Laker, he would find it difficult to stay healthy and it seemed like all the years of playing at an All-Star level had finally caught up to the 39-year old point guard.

Nash would only play until November before getting sidelined with nerve problems in his leg. On his 40th birthday, Nash got back on the court and scored 19 points in a win. 19 points was already impressive for any point guard let alone for a 40-year old former MVP. However, his season ended abruptly in March after his nerve problems resurfaced once again. He tried to return to the lineup after the Lakers lost Jordan Farmar to injury just to give the Lakers another point guard option. His last game for the season was on April 8, 2014, as he tallied 3 points and 5 assists in only 13 minutes of action. It would turn out that that was also Steve Nash's final regular season game in the NBA.

Retirement

Nash announced in July of 2014 that the 2014-15 season would be his last NBA year. He played three preseason games for the Lakers but his back problems resurfaced once again. Before the NBA season got going, Steve Nash was ruled out for the rest of the season as he could never really recover from that aggravated back injury. He voiced out his frustrations, as his only priority for his final year was to play the season and to try and support the Lakers as much as possible.[iv] It would have also been an opportunity for him to give NBA fans one last glimpse of the former two-time MVP. He never got back on the basketball court as an NBA player and retired immediately after the season ended.

After retiring, Steve Nash went on to work as a part-time consultant with the championship Golden State Warriors. He got to work with Steph Curry, a player who played a similar offensive style but did it on a higher pace than Nash ever did. He was approached by several teams for an attempt to make a comeback. These teams were the Cleveland Cavaliers and the Dallas Mavericks. Though they had legitimate championship chances (especially the Cavs), Nash declined due to his lingering injuries and out of respect for the purple and gold as he wanted to retire as a Laker.[v]

Chapter 5: International Career

Steve Nash also has some impressive international play under his belt. he was already playing for the Canadian Basketball Team as early as 1993, when he was still a college player in Santa Clara. Nash was instrumental in the Canadian National Basketball Team winning a silver medal in the Olympic qualifying tournament in Puerto Rico. Nash was named the tournament's Most Valuable Player. By placing second behind the United States, Team Canada earned a spot at the 2000 Summer Olympics in Sydney, Australia. Though Canada was eliminated in the quarterfinals, Steve Nash was optimistic about the loss, saying that Canada's improvement in the world stage could inspire more Canadians to play the sport at a very high level in order to make their country competitive in basketball.

Nash was once again named tournament MVP in the FIBA Americas Olympic Qualifying Tournament in 2004. However, Canada failed to make the Olympics after finishing the tournament at fourth place. That was the last time that Canada enjoyed the services of Steve Nash in their National Basketball team.

Chapter 6: Nash's Personal Life

There is a lot more to Steve Nash than just Steve Nash the basketball player. The NBA legend gives back to the community in several different ways and even has a few business ventures of his own.

Family Life

Steve Nash is the oldest of three children. His brother, Martin, is a professional Canadian soccer player who has played for the Canadian National Soccer Team on numerous occasions. His sister, Joann, played collegiate soccer in Canada.

While on a trip to Manhattan in 2001, Nash met and was immediately taken with Alejandra Amarilla. Alejandra became Steve Nash's girlfriend for a number of years. On October 14, 2004, Nash and Amarilla welcomed twin girls Lola and Belle into the world.

Nash tied the knot with his long-time girlfriend and the mother of his two children in June of 2005. The small family was happy together, and Nash was on his way to earning his first NBA Most Valuable Player award. Life was great for a number of years. On November 12, 2010, the couple welcomed a son, Matteo Joel, into the world. However, on the same day as the birth of his son, Steve Nash announced that he and Alejandra had split several months earlier, and were in the process of getting a divorce.

Health Issues

If you watch basketball regularly, you have probably seen Steve Nash lying on his team's bench during the little amount of time that he spends off the floor during a game. Steve suffers from a condition known as spondylolisthesis, which is a displacement of vertebrae. Spondylolisthesis causes muscles to tighten and to cramp up. Nash lies on the sidelines when he is out of the game to prevent his back from tightening up.

Philanthropic Efforts

Steve Nash is a well-known philanthropist. In 2006, Nash was named one of the 100 most influential people by *Time Magazine*. Around the NBA, Steve is known for being unselfish and caring. Nash once donated funds to a hospital in Paraguay to have a pediatric ward built.

Besides having been named one of the 100 most influential people in the world, Nash has also received a star of recognition on the Canadian Walk of Fame, and Canada's highest civilian honor known as The Order of Canada.

Nash also started the Steve Nash Foundation, which aims at helping young people in the Phoenix, Arizona, and the British Columbia areas. Because of his hard work and dedication to helping out the youth through the work of his foundation, Nash received an honorary law degree from the University of Victoria.

Steve also owns a Canadian fitness center that is modeled after his own fitness routine. Nash has been known to keep in great shape, which is one reason why he has been able to last so long in the NBA. In 2014, he was the only 40-year-old still active in the NBA. One of Nash's primary areas of focus is cardiovascular endurance.

Soccer's Influence on Steve

Steve Nash is an avid soccer fan. He has been known to tell people that he could have played professionally in soccer and he even worked out with some professional teams during the NBA offseason. Nash is a partial owner of the Vancouver Whitecaps FC, a professional soccer team in the British Columbia area. It is rumored that the reason Steve Nash and Dirk Nowitzki got along so well when they were teammates in Dallas was that they loved to watch soccer together during down time. Nash is known to be a supporter of several international soccer teams and was once given a jersey with his name on it from former teammate Leandro Barbosa's home team, Sport Club Corinthians Paulista.

Nash became the first NBA player to carry the torch and to light the Olympic Cauldron during the 2010 Vancouver Winter Olympics. He has also written and produced several television commercials.

Chapter 7: Nash's Legacy and Future

Though Nash was never able to win a title in his 18-year NBA career, he will undoubtedly leave a lasting legacy on the game of basketball. In 1996, the 6'3" Nash entered the NBA in what is often referred to as one of the most talented draft class ever. It was the same draft class that brought Allen Iverson and Kobe Bryant to the NBA. The class also had guys like Ray Allen, Ben Wallace, and Stephon Marbury. With all the talent in that draft class, Steve Nash, though unheralded, went on to win the most MVP awards of all the players drafted in 1996. Iverson and Bryant tied his two MVPs by winning the award once each.

Steve Nash has played in three eras of basketball. He played with the golden greats in the late 1990s, when he got a glimpse of what guys like Michael Jordan, John Stockton, and Karl Malone were like when they were dominating the NBA. Nash joined the NBA when Hall of Fame point guards like John Stockton were in the primes of their careers. He got to learn from one of the greatest eras in basketball history and there were several great point guards in the 90s. Other than Stockton, there were guys like Mark Jackson and Kevin Johnson.

Nash was also one of the best players in the 2000s, as he headlined the rank of the top NBA players together with guys like Kobe Bryant, Shaquille O'Neal, Tim Duncan, Kevin Garnett, and Dirk Nowitzki. He was instrumental in revitalizing the point guard position in an era when good point guards were scarce. Nash also brought back a high-octane, point guard-centered offense unseen since the time when Magic Johnson was dominating the league with his playmaking. With Nash at the helm of the Phoenix Suns, they were reminiscent of the "Showtime" Lakers in the 80s era.

And in the late 2000s up to the 2010s era, Nash saw an influx of talented point guards like Chris Paul, Derrick Rose, Stephen Curry, Russell Westbrook, and John Wall. The current era probably has the most superstar point guards in recent NBA history and Steve Nash was one of the players who inspired a whole generation of point guards to play the position at the highest level possible. He got to play against those rising point guards and several of those youngsters even idolized the two-time MVP when they were younger.

Nash was one of the main catalysts in revolutionizing the position of point guard during the new millennium. He brought new energy to the Phoenix Suns as the main instigator of their offense. The 2000s was also a decade in which point guards were rare. Hence, the best playmakers in that era were Nash and Jason Kidd. Both players led the league in assists and Nash was considered the best point guard of that era because of his ability to lead his team to victories just by passing and by being an efficient scorer.

While others like Russell Westbrook and Derrick Rose would revitalize the shoot-first, pass-second mentality starting in the late 2000s up to the current era of the NBA, Steve Nash was a refreshing reminder to basketball fans that pass-first point guards still could be highly effective in today's modern game of basketball. Today, guys like Rajon Rondo and John Wall have both taken pages from Nash's playbook. Players like them dominate games just by passing the ball. To some extent, Nash says that

Stephen Curry took off from where he left. Curry has a similar offensive game in that he can break defenses with ball handling instead of quickness and he can shoot the ball very efficiently. The difference, as Nash stated, is that Curry took what Nash did to a whole new level.[vi] Though Curry was never the playmaker that Nash was, his offensive game is a reminder of just how good Steve Nash was in his prime.

Playing in an era when point guards looked for their shot first and passed second, Nash embodied both worlds. Steve Nash had over 17,000 career points and 10,000 career assists. He always showed an exemplary amount of skill passing the basketball, being able to thread the ball in and out of traffic to fellow stars like Amar'e Stoudemire. He electrified spectators and made big men look like MVPs on the basketball court, throwing alley-oop passes long before Chris Paul began tossing alley-oops to Blake Griffin in Lob City. He was pulling up for three-point baskets from far beyond the three-point line way before Steph Curry lit up buildings with his prolific three-point shooting. He was breaking ankles nearly a decade before Kyrie Irving started losing defenders with his slick ball handling. Steve Nash was simply a revolutionary and paved the way for today's point guards to excel in the NBA.

Nash did a lot for the game of basketball and the city of Phoenix. Nash was the architect of the "seven seconds or less" offense that was run by the Suns throughout the mid-2000s, making them one of the most exciting teams to watch at the time. Phoenix loved Nash as much as he loved Phoenix and its basketball fans. Nash helped the Suns make many playoff appearances and deep playoff runs. Although the Suns never capitalized on those appearances by winning a championship, Steve Nash made Phoenix a legitimate playoff contender year in and year out. While Nash revolutionized the way the game was played, overall, some of his biggest impact on the city of Phoenix happened off the court.

While Nash's incredible run with the Phoenix Suns never resulted in a championship, hindsight has shown just how large a role he played as the leader of the team. Coach Mike D'Antoni was frequently praised for his "seven seconds and less" offense. But after D'Antoni left the

Phoenix Suns in 2008, he has been largely unable to replicate the same success that he had coaching Steve Nash. Shawn Marion never made the All-Star team after being traded to Miami in 2008. Amar'e Stoudemire signed with the New York Knicks in 2010. Thanks to injuries, today he barely belongs in this league despite being just in his mid 30s. And even when a different coach was at the helm of the Suns, Steve Nash was still able to get his numbers and translate games into victories. It was Nash who made those players and coaches look good and they seemed so dominant because of the point guard's ability to make plays for them.

Throughout Nash's time with the Suns, it was commonly asserted that Nash was only successful because he had excellent teammates like Stoudemire and Marion around him. But as we look back, it seems clear that those teammates appeared so good because Nash made them excellent, just as a great point guard is supposed to do. After those teammates left Nash, they were largely unable to replicate the success they found in Phoenix. And even without All-Star caliber teammates, Nash was still enjoying All-Star appearances by racking up the assists. If anything, Nash made those players successful. It was not the other way around.

Steve Nash founded the Steve Nash Foundation to help youths in his native British Columbia and in Phoenix. The Steve Nash Foundation provides services to at-risk youths in the Phoenix area, addressing the needs of youths all over the city and helping keep these youths off the street. For his actions while a resident of Phoenix, Nash received the NBA's citizenship award. Through the Steve Nash Foundation, Nash's legacy off the basketball court and to the city of Phoenix will last long after he has retired from the game of basketball.

With his contributions to Phoenix on and off the court, Steve Nash is probably the best player in franchise history. Though he was never a high-profile scorer, Nash ranks seventh among the highest scorers in Suns history. He is the top overall three-point shooter with over 1051 makes as a Sun. His 6997 career assists with the Suns is also the highest in franchise history, as he leads Kevin Johnson by over 400 assists. Best of all, he was able to deliver two

MVP awards to the Valley of the Rising Sun. No other Suns player in the history of the franchise can say that they did the same for the team.

Nash currently stands third on the all-time assists list, two spots ahead of Magic Johnson and one assist higher than Mark Jackson. While Jason Kidd is second on the list, basketball fans should keep in mind that Nash spent two seasons sitting behind Kidd when he was a young player in Phoenix. Nash, like Kidd, is a player who, despite being capable of scoring at will, always looked to pass the ball first. Nash helped bring back the run-and-gun offense, in which a team takes advantage of their physical conditioning by moving the ball quickly and getting the ball into the hands of a player who has a high percentage shot. Throughout his career, Nash had seven double-double seasons where he averaged more than 10 points and more than 10 assists per game.

Steve Nash retired from the NBA as the league's all-time free throw percentage leader, hitting over 90% of his shots from the charity stripe. Shooting 90% from the charity stripe is no easy feat. Steve Nash's impressive free-throw shooting percentage made him one of the last players a team would want to foul down the stretch in a close game.

What Legacy Does Nash Leave the Future?

Nash has helped inspire future NBA guards and how they will play in the years to come. He made passing ability cool again. His ability to pass from anywhere on the basketball court has shown future generations of NBA players that you do not have to score every time you touch the ball to make an impact in the game because it is also imperative as a point guard to make other players look good by making easy plays for them. Nash has shown the world that smart shot selection is of the utmost importance. He was always a very efficient shooter and rarely missed from the floor. Although, he did not win a championship, he was part of some of the highest-scoring and fastest-moving offenses that have ever taken the court at the highest level.

Steve Nash also leads the NBA in most career 50-40-90 seasons. The 50-40-90 club is exclusive for those players who have shot over 50% from the floor, 40% from the three-point line, and 90% from the charity stripe in a regular season. Steve Nash has done it four times. The only other player who has done it more than once is the legendary Larry Bird with two 50-40-90 seasons. Only four other players have accomplished that feat and two of them, Dirk Nowitzki and Kevin Durant, are actively playing. What this means for Nash is that he is one of the most efficient players in NBA history. While he was never a high-profile scorer, he scored enough to help his team win and, when he attempted to score, he was always efficient. With his shooting efficiency, Steve Nash is ranked among the best shooters in NBA history.

Although Steve Nash was known for his pass first-shoot second mentality, he also has a fundamentally sound shooting motion. In college, Nash was deemed the most complete college point guard in the United States since he could shoot and pass from anywhere, though he was not as explosive in scoring as Allen Iverson and Stephon Marbury were.

Some critics have argued that Nash is not among the best to ever play his position, but then you must look at what he has done for the game of basketball. Steve Nash stands at the top all-time in two categories: 50-40-90 seasons and career free throw percentage. Nash is in the top five all-time in career assists with the likes of Jason Kidd, Magic Johnson, and John Stockton. The only point that anyone can make when arguing that Nash is not among the best to ever play his position is that he does not have a championship ring. While that is true, you cannot discount what he has done over the course of his career. And we can never blame him for his lack of championships either because he was playing in a very competitive 2000s era dominated by the Los Angeles Lakers and the San Antonio Spurs, both of which have multiple superstars.

Nash's MVP seasons were also not without criticism. When he won his first Most Valuable Player award in 2005, he got a lot of criticism as he only averaged 15.5 points and 11.5 assists that year. Meanwhile, the runner-up Shaquille O'Neal was a virtual 20-10 guy in scoring and rebounding and he changed the Miami Heat from a cellar-dwelling team into a contender. But in Nash's case, he was also a game-changer for the Suns, who were not even close to being a playoff team the previous years. In his second MVP season, nobody was close to the votes he garnered but people still believed he did not deserve the award because a guy in LA named Kobe Bryant was putting up 35 points a night. But Nash deserved every bit of that second MVP because he led the Suns into the playoffs without their leading scorer, Amar'e Stoudemire.

With all of his accomplishments during the course of his long career, which has spanned from the mid 1990s to 2014, one thing that Steve Nash never did was play outside his means. Nash has never been one to talk trash since he did his talking through his play on the court. Perhaps the biggest thing that Steve Nash will leave to Phoenix, to basketball, and to the world as a whole is first and foremost that he was one of the classiest players in the NBA and a true example of good sportsmanship. Secondly, Steve Nash is a perfect example of hard work and perseverance. Nash decided as a child that he was going to play in the NBA. Yet, nobody gave him a chance since he was just a skinny kid from British Columbia. The big colleges did not want him. Despite the numerous rejections he received from some of the notable basketball schools in the nation, he persevered and continued to play. When he arrived at Santa Clara he continued to work hard and made it to the NBA, never giving up on his goal. Steve Nash's life and career is a true testament to what hard work and dedication can do for you.

When all is said and done, Steve Nash will be remembered as not just a great basketball player, but as a man as well. Steve Nash is a dedicated philanthropist who gave and continues to give back to his city. He will be remembered for the way he beat all of the odds not only by making it to the NBA, but for how hard he continued to work once he made it to the NBA. Steve Nash will be remembered not only for setting records, but also for the way he played to earn those records.

Steve Nash is one of the greats and he will be forever remembered as such. Looking over the course of his career, there is no doubt that Steve Nash will be a first-ballot Hall of Famer. And we'll be expecting his name enshrined in the Naismith Basketball Hall of Fame in a few years to come.

Final Word/About the Author

I was born and raised in Norwalk, Connecticut. Growing up, I could often be found spending many nights watching basketball, soccer, and football matches with my father in the family living room. I love sports and everything that sports can embody. I believe that sports are one of most genuine forms of competition, heart, and determination. I write my works to learn more about influential athletes in the hopes that from my writing, you the reader can walk away inspired to put in an equal if not greater amount of hard work and perseverance to pursue your goals. If you enjoyed *Steve Nash: The Inspiring Story of One of Basketball's Greatest Point Guards,* please leave a review! Also, you can read more of my works on *Colin Kaepernick, Aaron Rodgers, Peyton Manning, Tom Brady, Russell Wilson, Michael Jordan, LeBron James, Kyrie Irving, Klay Thompson, Stephen Curry, Kevin Durant, Russell Westbrook, Anthony Davis, Chris Paul, Blake Griffin, Kobe Bryant, Joakim Noah, Scottie Pippen, Carmelo Anthony, Kevin Love, Grant Hill, Tracy McGrady, Vince Carter, Patrick Ewing, Karl Malone,*

Tony Parker, Allen Iverson, Hakeem Olajuwon, Reggie Miller, Michael Carter-Williams, John Wall, James Harden, Tim Duncan, Pau Gasol and *Marc Gasol* in the Kindle Store. If you love basketball, check out my website at claytongeoffreys.com to join my exclusive list where I let you know about my latest books and give you lots of goodies.

Like what you read? Please leave a review!

I write because I love sharing the stories of influential people like Steve Nash with fantastic readers like you. My readers inspire me to write more so please do not hesitate to let me know what you thought by leaving a review! If you love books on life, basketball, or productivity, check out my website at claytongeoffreys.com to join my exclusive list where I let you know about my latest books. Aside from being the first to hear about my latest releases, you can also download a free copy of *33 Life Lessons: Success Principles, Career Advice & Habits of Successful People*. See you there!

Clayton

References

[i] Bedard, Phil. "Steve Nash Scouting Report". *Ibibilio*. Web

[ii] Smith, Russ. "Steve Nash Scouting Report". *Ibibilio*. Web

[iii] Bedard, Phil. "Steve Nash Scouting Report". *Ibibilio*. Web

[iv] "Steve Nash Out For the Season". *NBA.com*. 23 October 2014. Web

[v] Stein, Marc, "How Nash Found Peace with Retirement". *ESPN*. 22 March 2015. Web

[vi] Herbert, James. "Steve Nash on Stephen Curry: 'He's taken what I did to another level.'" *CBSSports*. 19 November 2015. Web

15441166R00066

Printed in Great Britain
by Amazon